Preface

HACCP is used in food businesses as a preventive appr〔...〕ood. Food safety and quality management systems (FS〔...〕s is a fundamental requirement of All GFSI recognised food 〔...〕

For the development of a successful HACCP plan this book has been divided into two parts: Part A & Part B

Part A gives a precise detailed picture of how to begin with HACCP plan from scratch in real world of food manufacturing while in part B a step by step HACCP plan development shown using real food manufacturing product as an example for practical explanation.

	CONTENTS	Page No
PART A	HAZARD ANALYSIS & CRITICAL CONTROL POINT SITE INTRODUCTION	5
	SCOPE of the HACCP	6
	HACCP STEPS & PRINCIPLES	7
	PRE-REQUISITES	8
	LEGISLATION & CODES OF PRACTICE	9
	EXAMPLES of Hazards	10
	SUMMARY SITE CCP's	12
	SITE DOCUMENTATION & RECORDS	13
	VALIDATION & VERIFICATION	14
	SITE HACCP SUMMARY PLANS	15
PART B	A Real Practical HACCP Development	16-49

British Institute of Food Safety and Industrial Training, BIFSIT

Part A
SCOPE OF THE HACCP

(Business Name) food safety plan is based on a HACCP system which is systematic, comprehensive, thorough, fully implemented and maintained.
In order to achieve this, (Business Name)

1. Completed a full Hazard Analysis investigation on all our process and product groups following the Codex Alimentarius HACCP principles.
2. Construct quality systems to ensure that all the hazards which are identified as critical are controlled
3. Established a supporting pre-requisite system
4. Staff training
5. Review and verify the effectiveness of these systems on a regular basis.
6. Contract review and customer focus
7. Conduct a Hazard Analysis exercise on all new products.
8. All HACCP studies are carried out and reviewed by the multidisciplinary HACCP team which will comprise of :

Role	Title	Name	Qualifications
Team Leader	Technical Manager	xxx Name xxx	HACCP Level 3
Team Member	Managing Director	xxx Name xxx	HACCP Level 2
Team Member	Production Manager	xxx Name xxx	HACCP Level 2
Team Member	Hygiene Manager	xxx Name xxx	HACCP Level2
Team Member	Engineering Manager	xxx Name xxx	HACCP Level 2

(Business Name) manufactures a range of tray bakes, xxx, sweet & savoury xxx, cheesecakes etc. These are produced using prepared cooked pastry and sponge bases that are creatively assembled from pre-blended and mixed ingredients, finished with design, chilled or frozen prior to despatch.

Products are produced own label for the xxx customer xxx

(Business Name) have identified the need for xxx (enter number of processes) process HACCP plans

British Institute of Food Safety and Industrial Training, BIFSIT

HACCP STEPS AND PRINCIPLES

(Business Name) use a systematic & comprehensive system which follows the Codex Alimentarius HACCP twelve steps and seven principles for each HACCP plan identified and implemented on site:

Codex Alimentarius Step 1 – HACCP FOOD SAFETY TEAM

Codex Alimentarius Step 2 – DESCRIPTION OF THE PRODUCT

Codex Alimentarius Step 3 – IDENTIFIED INTENDED USE

Codex Alimentarius Step 4 – CONSTRUCT A PROCESS FLOW

Codex Alimentarius Step 5 - VERIFY THE FLOW

Codex Alimentarius Step 6 – *PRINICPLE 1* - Conduct a hazard analysis

Codex Alimentarius Step 7 – *PRINCIPLE 2* - Determine the Critical Control Points (CCPs).

Codex Alimentarius Step 8 – *PRINCIPLE 3* - Establish critical limits.

Codex Alimentarius Step 9 – *PRINCIPLE 4* - Establish a system to monitor control of the CCP.

Codex Alimentarius Step 10 – *PRINCIPLE 5* - Establish the corrective action to be taken when monitoring indicates that a particular CCP is not under control.

Codex Alimentarius Step 11 – *PRINCIPLE 6* - Establish procedures of validation and verification to confirm that the HACCP system is working effectively.

Codex Alimentarius Step 12 – *PRINCIPLE 7* - Establish documentation concerning all procedures and records appropriate to these principles and their application.

British Institute of Food Safety and Industrial Training, BIFSIT

PRE-REQUISITES

Pre-requisites, which are the on site supporting system to the HACCP and are referenced within each of the HACCP plans, have been identified as:

Glass and Brittle Material Control
Water
Pest Control
Cleaning and Hygiene
Calibration
Site Temperature Control
Transport Policy
Personal and Protective Clothing
Allergen Policy & Segregation
Medical Screening
Supplier & Raw Material Quality Assurance
Traceability
Waste Control
Animal Food "Waste"
Site Hygiene & Housekeeping Rules
Maintenance Policy
Staff Training
Pest Control
Genetically Modified Organisms
Work in Progress
Re-work Policy
Physical Contamination, including Metal and Wood Policy

These are formally documented and controlled by the Quality Management System.

LEGISLATIVE STANDARDS, REGULATIONS AND CODES OF PRACTICE
(for UK Based Industry)

Food Safety Act 1990

Food labelling (Declaration of Allergens) 2007 and subsequent amendments

The Pesticides regulations 2007

Food Labelling Regulations 1996

Food Safety regulations (General Food Hygiene) 1995

The Food Safety (Temperature Control) Regulations 1995

Weights and Measures Act 1985

Water Supply (Water Quality) Regulations 2000
Weights and Measures (Packaged goods) Regs 2006

The plastic materials & articles in contact with food regs 2008

The Microbiological Criteria for Foodstuffs Regulation 2006

Criteria for the use of food labeling terms (eg Pure, Fresh, Natural)

Guidance on vegetarian and vegan food labeling

Allergen Labelling Directive 2003/89/EC of 10 November 2003

Genetically Modified and Novel food ingredients regulations 2000

Bread and Flour regulations

Trade Descriptions Act 1968

The Consumer Protection Act 1987

The Prices Act 1974

Food Additives Legislation Guidance notes

Sources of information:

- *Food Standards Agency*
- *Local Trading standards office*
- *Local Environmental standards office*

British Institute of Food Safety and Industrial Training, BIFSIT

- *We are members of (put accreditation running body name)*
- *Internet*

Compliance with Codes of Practice
Quality Management System

EXAMPLES OF HAZARDS

Only food safety hazards are to be considered in the HACCP studies (to include biological, chemical and physical hazards (or any combination of these) in the food

Microbiological: (Presence/Introduction/Growth/Survival)
Spoilage
Yeast
Moulds
Pathogens

Enterobacteriaceae

Salmonella Spp

Staphylococcus aureus (*and their toxin*s)

Listeria Monocytogenes

E-Coli

Bacillus cereus (and their *spores & toxins)*

Clostridium perfringens (*and their spores*)

Physical:
Hair
Glass, brittle plastic or ceramic

Wood

People

String

Cardboard

Packaging Materials

Old Product/dough

Metal

Paint

Belt and equipment Fibres

Pests; SPI (store product insects), rodents, mice

Chemical:

Oil & Grease

Cleaning Materials

Inks and taints from packaging and labelling

Mycotoxins (Aflatoxins/Ochratoxins)

Pesticide Residue

Allergens: *Wheat Gluten, Soya, Egg, Milk, Nuts, Sesame*

	Site HACCP Critical Control Point Summary
CCP 1	*Xxx ccp name xxx*
CCP 2	*Xxx ccp name xxx*
CCP 3	*Xxx ccp name xxx*
CCP 4	*Xxx ccp name xxx*

British Institute of Food Safety and Industrial Training, BIFSIT

(Business Name) Documentation & Records for the sites HACCP

Due diligence and food safety records include:

Goods inwards inspection form

Temperature Monitoring forms

Traceability Forms

Non-Conformance Form

Glass & Brittle Materials audit form (Daily, Weekly, and Monthly)

Personal Hygiene and Swabbing form

Hygiene & Housekeeping Audits

Calibration Records

Training Records

Cooking and Cooling Batch forms

Risk Assessment Forms

Metal Detection

Planned Maintenance records

Pest Control

Cleaning Schedules and Forms

HACCP Validation/Verification

HACCP Review/Verification

British Institute of Food Safety and Industrial Training, BIFSIT

Knife Control

Micro Analysis Schedule

Internal Audits

HACCP VALIDATION AND VERIFICATION

VALIDATION

To ensure the HACCP flow diagram (Codex Step N°5) and system is suitable and accurate (Validation) and to ensure and measure the effectiveness of the HACCP system (Verification) it needs to be regularly monitored and audited. (codex Step 11 principle 6)
This includes the following:

1) Completion of the **Validation form PCS xxx** on flow compliance and plan implementation.

2) Internal Auditing – trained independent auditor (2nd party).

3) Third party verification followed by an external audit or assessment. (Customer, Accreditation body, law enforcement/regulators bodies)

4) Monthly customer complaint analysis

5) CCP auditing weekly check list

- Any non-conformities or adverse trends in deviation would result in an investigation, follow up audit and/or amendments/implementations to the system.
- Results from this validation/verification process is carried out and communicated on a Management meeting and the completion of form **PCS xxx**

REVIEW & VERIFICATION (Codex Step No.11 Principle 6)

This includes any of the following:

1) New Product Development, including packaging changes

2) Process Change, equipment or layout change

3) Increase in customer complaints or product incident (food safety – recall)

4) Change in Raw Material/Supplier

5) Change in consumer use of product

6) Development in scientific or legislative information associated with ingredients,

Process or product

- Results of the above are documented onto the **Review/Verification form PCS xxx**- Annual review & verification is necessary to ensure all aspects of the HACCP are effective and this is carried out by a second or third party independent auditor on completion on **Review/Verification form PCS xxx**
- Results from this verification process is carried out and communicated on a regular basis at the monthly Management meeting.

Part - B

In this chapter a step by step HACCP plan will be developed using pastry product as an example for practical explanation purpose.

HACCP PLAN (XXX)

BUSINESS NAME:
BUSINESS ADDRESS: xxx..... xxx Tel xxx....xxx

British Institute of Food Safety and Industrial Training, BIFSIT

HACCP STUDY FOR (PROCESS):

(———-) Manufacture

DATE OF PREPARATION: DDMMYYYY

CODEX ALIMENTARIUS STEP 1

HACCP TEAM	DATE: January 2011
TEAM LEADER: Role in Company	(-----) Technical Manager
Team Member 1: Role in Company	(-------) Factory Manager
Team Member 2: Role in Company	(-------) Production Manager
Team Member 3: Role in Company	

British Institute of Food Safety and Industrial Training, BIFSIT

Team Member 4:		
Role in Company		
Other Inputs by:		

CODEX ALIMENTARIUS STEP 2 & 3

HACCP PLAN FOR: MANUFACTURE OF SPONGE BASES, DANISH, MUFFINS, BISCUITS & PUDDINGS
The receipt of raw materials and semi-processed products (Danish, XXX, Pastries) which are batch weighed, blended OR prepared in readiness for baking, chilling and either packing ready for chilled or frozen despatch OR used as a sub-component for the assembly of Cakes, Gateaux & mousses for HACCP Plan (XXX).

This HACCP plan was prepared by: (------)
Date of preparation: MMYYYY

Scope of the hazards:

Microbiological Safety:
The main aim of this HACCP study is to avoid the **presence** of bacteria on raw material arrival, avoid the **introduction** of significant levels of microbiological contamination onto the product, to reduce the potential for **growth** and principally through maintaining the temperature during raw material storage and avoid the **survival** through the baking process.

Physical Safety:
To avoid the introduction of physical foreign bodies

Chemical Safety:
To avoid the introduction via contamination of chemical taints or residue, awareness of allergens present and risk of cross contamination onto the product

Sponges, XXX, Puddings Manufacture HACCP Plan (XXX)

Raw materials, semi-processed materials and packaging that are delivered for the purpose of sponges, brownies etc arrive frozen, chilled and ambient and are delivered at the unit under temperature controlled hygienic transport from approved suppliers.
All materials are immediately inspected prior to off loading and results are recorded on the Goods Inward sheet. On quality and safety compliance all items are placed in the Freezer, Chiller or Ambient dry stores area with separation of product prior to processing.
Upon receipt of orders, the raw material items are deboxed prior to entering the factory and follow one or more of the following processes carried out on site, prior to the assembly of the finished products.
1. DEFROSTING/TEMPERING – Those materials that require defrosting prior to cooking or assembly, which include semi-processed purchased items including danishes, biscuits, & puff pastry are transferred to the chiller

where the primary packaging is removed, if applicable and placed into covered labelled trays. Label with Product, Traceability, DOP + use by 3 days. Temperature monitoring is carried out until the temperature of reaches >0°c.

2. PREPARATION – (Blending/Mixing) - All the pre-prepared and de-boxed/debagged raw materials are transferred to the low care production area for blending. The ingredients are batch weighed against a recipe and each traceability code and temperature is recorded. The ingredients are blended in the mixer and immediately transferred for deposit into tins/trays ready for cooking. Pastry prepared (as below), Biscuits, Muffins Danish's, Brownies are trayed and some may be proved prior to baking

3. PASTRY PREPARATION & BAKING- Pre-purchased prepared pastry (ie apple tarts), after tempering, is transferred to the low care for cutting and forming into the various bases and shapes. The pastry are baked in the oven at variable oven temperature and time (refer to recipes) to achieve a core temperature of >82°c for 30 secs. The cooked pastry is placed into the chiller for cooling to <8°c within 90 mins until required.

4. PROOVING – Croissants, Danish's, and pastry is proved for 30-35°c for 40 mins to achieve correct shape and size through rising.

5. BAKING – Finished product traceability code is applied to the sheet and silicon lined tray used to hold the products ready for baking. Each tray is stacked, labelled with product and traceability details and transferred to the oven for baking. The baking times are variable due to product type (refer to recipe) but all to achieve a core temperature >82°c for 30 secs. Those products considered perishable are immediately transferred to the chiller for cooling <8°c within 90 mins. Sponges, brownies and those items with low Aw are ambient cooled

6. POST BAKING FURTHER PREPARATIONS. Biscuits, puddings, danish pastries may be glazed or topped, chilled and packed ready for despatch and Sponge bases are further processed in **HACCP Plan (XXX)**

PACKING & STORAGE

Those items that are considered finished products are either trayed, sleeved or boxed into lined outer cases and labelled, if applicable with Product, DOP + 3 - 17 days life chilled or ambient OR DOP + 12 months if frozen. Some customers are palletised if applicable. Items are immediately transferred to the freezer for freezing to <-18°c, best practice to achieve <-12°c within 36hrs or chiller prior to despatch or customer collection.

The premises maintain temperature control in the chillers and freezers with automatic digital read out screens. On site chillers and freezers are continuously monitored and controlled to reduce the risk of any microbial growth on site, and the product and air temperature is regularly physically monitored with a calibrated temperature probe. Chillers run between 0-5°c and Freezer are held at -23°c to maintain a product temperature <-18°c.

ANALYSIS

Each batch of finished product is assessed for quality either on the day of, the day after production, or held for 3 days after production due to the weekend. Results are assessed against specification, passed/rejected and recorded.

Finished product microbiological analysis is carried out routinely every month. (BusinessName) holds historical and scientific data on their products produced. Any product out of specification will be put on hold or discarded as appropriate.

DISTRIBUTION AND THIRD PARTY STORAGE

Product is despatch by unit in trays by our own refrigerated vehicle that is regularly monitored for temperature and hygiene and (customers names) a Fresh Direct distribution services.

Details of intended use and customer.
A full list of the end product is available from the office, on-line and via our brochure but also includes: (customers names)

Suitability of Vulnerable Groups:
The target populations include adults and children but may include children and the elderly. Products are consumed ready to eat (unless defrosting is required) without any further cooking process.
The case label and finished product specification details, the intended use which could include the defrost method times & temperatures, storage and handling conditions, the use by date of 3 – 14 days chilled or BB date frozen of 12 months. Ingredients declaration and any allergen safety information.
Suitability of Vulnerable Groups: As determined through risk (reference FSA guidelines)
Allergens CONTAINS: **Wheat Gluten, Egg, Cow's Milk, Nuts, Seeds, Soy** (Products that contain Chocolate)

British Institute of Food Safety and Industrial Training, BIFSIT

A comprehensive list of allergen by product is available in the site FSQM.
MAY CONTAINS: TBC by risk assessment.
Risk Group Category: Medium - High.
(Business Name) currently declares all allergens that are handled on site for each product label produced.

CODEX ALIMENTARIUS STEP 4

Process Flow Diagram for: MANUFACTURE OF SPONGE BASES, xxx & PUDDINGS

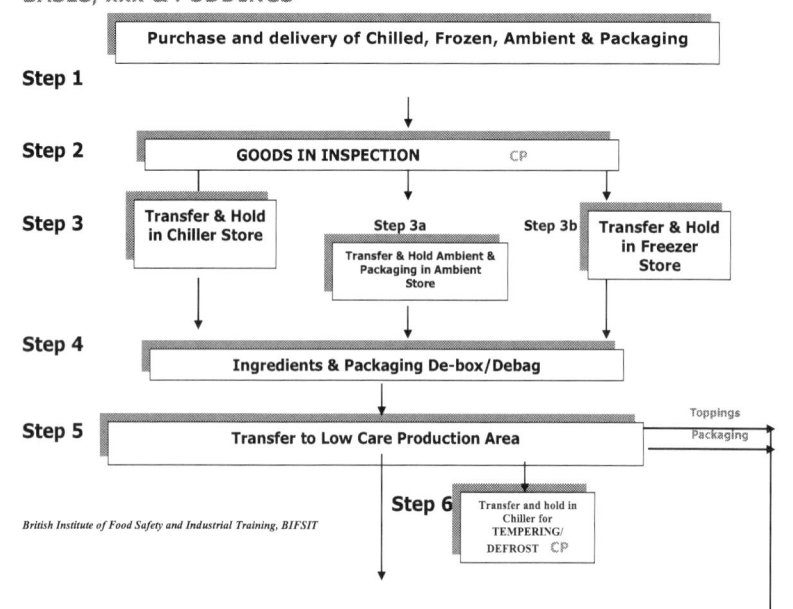

Step 1: Purchase and delivery of Chilled, Frozen, Ambient & Packaging

Step 2: GOODS IN INSPECTION — CP

Step 3: Transfer & Hold in Chiller Store

- Step 3a: Transfer & Hold Ambient & Packaging in Ambient Store
- Step 3b: Transfer & Hold in Freezer Store

Step 4: Ingredients & Packaging De-box/Debag

Step 5: Transfer to Low Care Production Area → Toppings, Packaging

Step 6: Transfer and hold in Chiller for TEMPERING/ DEFROST — CP

British Institute of Food Safety and Industrial Training, BIFSIT

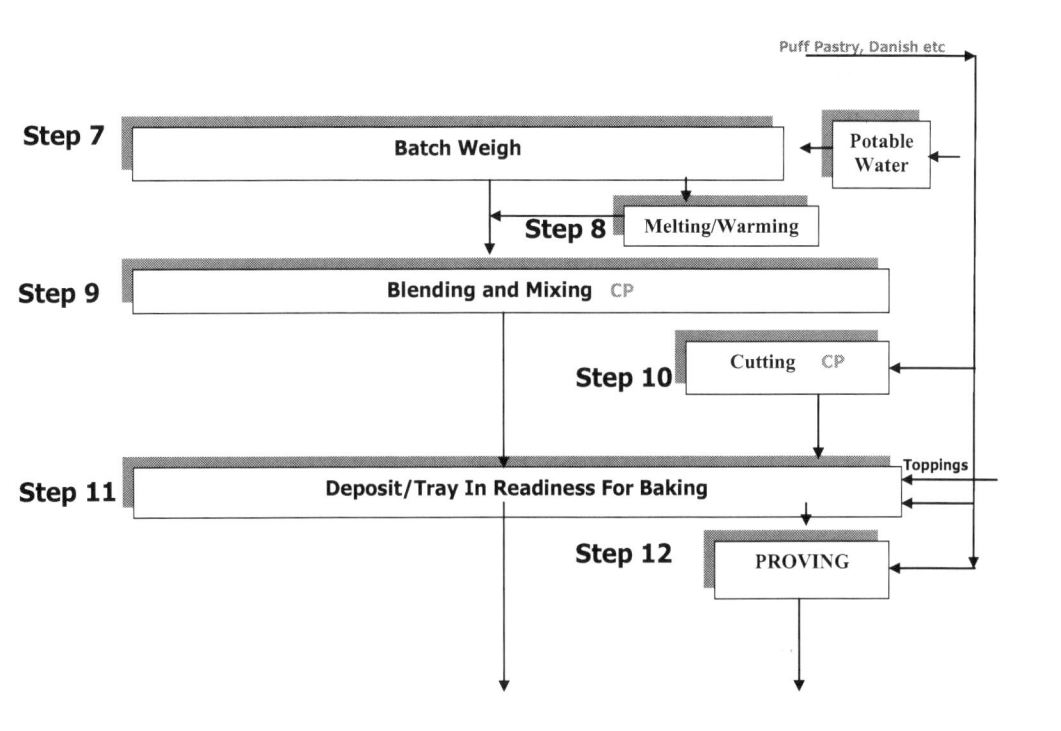

Puff Pastry, Danish etc

Step 7 — Batch Weigh ← Potable Water

Step 8 — Melting/Warming

Step 9 — Blending and Mixing CP

Step 10 — Cutting CP

Toppings

Step 11 — Deposit/Tray In Readiness For Baking

Step 12 — PROVING

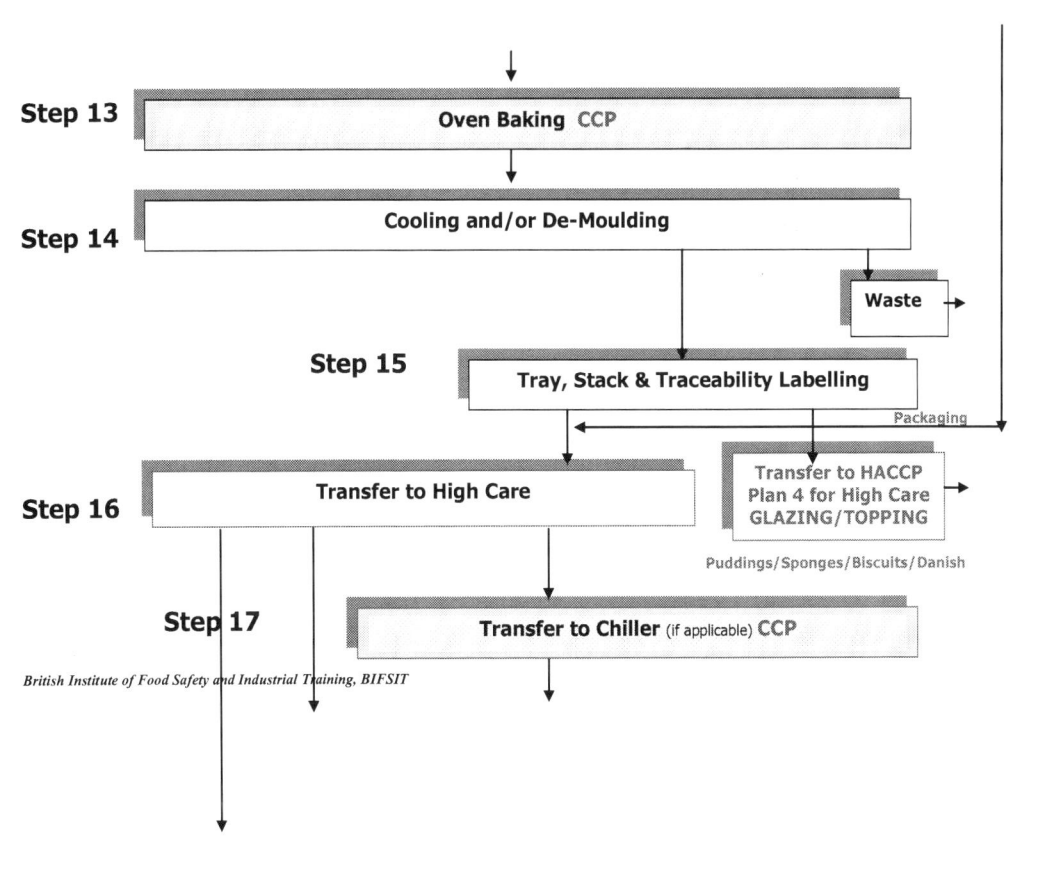

Step 13 — Oven Baking CCP

Step 14 — Cooling and/or De-Moulding → Waste

Step 15 — Tray, Stack & Traceability Labelling

Packaging

Step 16 — Transfer to High Care

Transfer to HACCP Plan 4 for High Care GLAZING/TOPPING

Puddings/Sponges/Biscuits/Danish

Step 17 — Transfer to Chiller (if applicable) CCP

British Institute of Food Safety and Industrial Training, BIFSIT

Step 18 — Cutting/Slicing (if applicable)

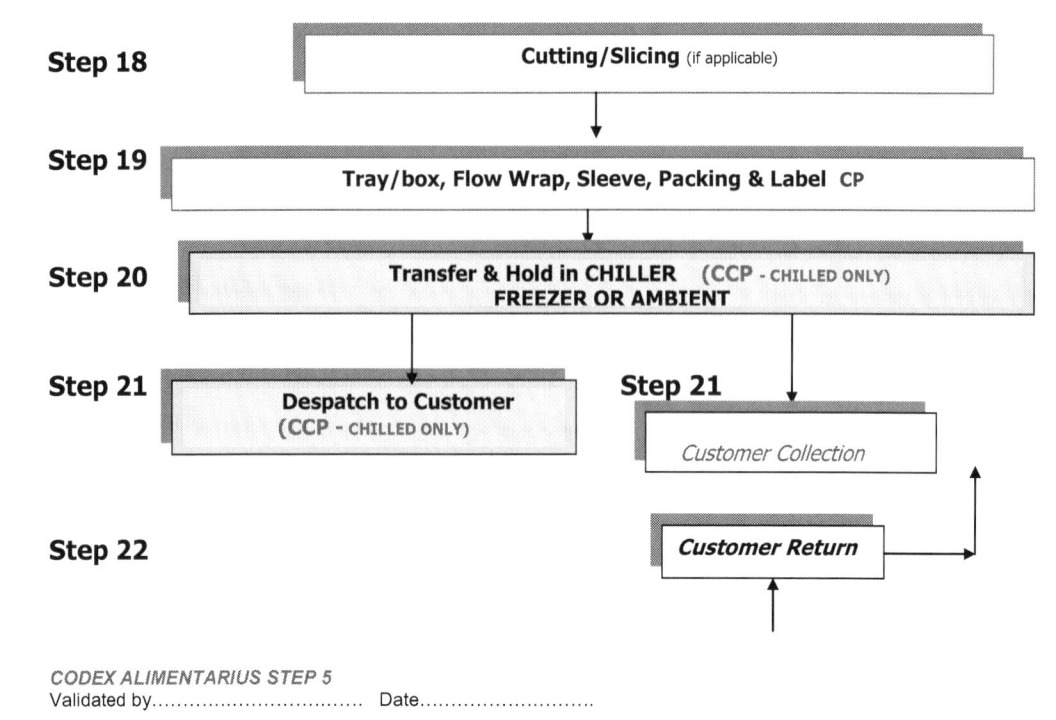

Step 19 — Tray/box, Flow Wrap, Sleeve, Packing & Label CP

Step 20 — Transfer & Hold in CHILLER (CCP - CHILLED ONLY) FREEZER OR AMBIENT

Step 21 — Despatch to Customer (CCP - CHILLED ONLY)

Step 21 — *Customer Collection*

Step 22 — *Customer Return*

CODEX ALIMENTARIUS STEP 5
Validated by……………………….…… Date………………………..

British Institute of Food Safety and Industrial Training, BIFSIT

CODEX ALIMENTARIUS STEP 6 PRINCIPLE 1
HAZARD ANALYSIS

Step	Process Step	Hazard(s) Micro (including toxins), Chemical & Physical	Control Measures	Pre-requisite Y/N
1	Purchase & Delivery (Flour, Sugar, margarine, Egg, Dairy, Raw Danish, Pastry, Biscuits, Fruits, Yeast, Pre-mixes, Packaging)	*REFER TO LTD SITE RAW MATERIAL & RISK ASSESSMENT FILE FOR DETAILS BY INGREDIENT* **Microbiological** (Spoilage; Yeast and Moulds /Pathogens: Salmonella spp., Listeria monocytogenes, Bacillus cereus, Enterobacteriaceae, Staphylococcus aureus, E.coli 1057, Clostridium perfingens, Coliforms, and their toxins) - **Presence of** Spoilage & Pathogens due to supplier process & handling, despatch and insufficient controls on site and transport delivery. - **Growth of** pathogens due to loss of temperature and controls during transportation - **Introduction by Contamination** of Staphylococcus from people. **Physical Contamination** Including foreign bodies from Metal, Wood, String, Plastic, Paper, Egg Shell, Vegetable matter, Dirt/Grit, Paper/Cardboard, Glass & Brittle Material, Pests, including beetle/insects (SPI'S) from supplier chain, site, People & supplier transport vehicle **Chemical Contamination** **Cleaning chemical** taint residue from supplier site and supplier transport vehicle **Deliberate Allergens** : Wheat Gluten, Egg, Milk, Nuts, Soy, Seeds, Peanuts **Allergen risk of Cross contamination** from other products during supplier processing, handling and during transportation **Mycotoxins (Aflotoxins/Ochratoxins)** from Wheat Crops *(considered only at this point due to supplier chain controls)* **Rancidity** due to insufficient supplier processing and handling controls **Chemical Ink Solvents taints** from packaging	*REFER TO LTD SITE RAW MATERIAL & RISK ASSESSMENT FILE FOR DETAILS BY INGREDIENT* Chilled delivery temperature conditions: 0 - 5°C. Product temperature maintained during delivery <5°C. Frozen delivery temperature conditions <-18°c Product temperature maintained during delivery <-18°c Purchase from approved raw material and packaging suppliers Supplier Self Questionnaire & allergen cross contamination questionnaire completed and assessed for compliance Routine Supplier Audits Raw Material Specifications Certificate of Analysis/conformance per batch, if applicable All products appropriately labelled with name, product, batch use by/BB & traceability coding. Correct Stock rotation Vehicle breakdown procedure and hygiene and transportation policy and procedures. Allergen labelling identification and separation.	Y Y

HAZARD ANALYSIS

Step	Process Step	Hazard(s) Micro (including toxins), Chemical & Physical	Control Measures	Pre-requisite Y/N
2	Inspection	**REFER TO LTD SITE RAW MATERIAL & RISK ASSESSMENT FILE FOR DETAILS BY INGREDIENT** **Microbiological** (Spoilage; Yeast and Moulds /Pathogens: Salmonella spp., Listeria monocytogenes, Bacillus cereus, Enterobacteriaceae, Staphylococcus aureus, E.coli 1057, Clostridium perfingens, Coliforms, and their toxins) - **Presence of** Spoilage & Pathogens due to supplier process & handling, despatch and insufficient controls on site and transport delivery. - **Growth of** pathogens due to loss of temperature and controls during transportation and at the point of inspection - **Introduction by Contamination** of Staphylococcus from people during delivery/inspection point at site **Physical Contamination** Including foreign bodies from Metal, Wood, String, Plastic, Paper, Egg Shell, Vegetable matter, Dirt/Grit, Paper/Cardboard, Glass & Brittle Material, Pests, including beetle/insects (SPI'S) from supplier chain, site, People & supplier transport vehicle Product Lumps due to insufficient supplier site processing, handling and transport environment controls **Chemical Contamination** **Cleaning chemical** taint residue from supplier site and supplier transport vehicle **Deliberate Allergens** : Wheat Gluten, Egg, Milk, Nuts, Soy, Seeds, Peanuts **Allergen risk of Cross contamination** from other products during supplier processing, handling, during transportation and at delivery inspection point. **Rancidity** due to insufficient supplier processing and handling controls **Chemical Ink Solvents taints** from packaging	**REFER TO LTD SITE RAW MATERIAL & RISK ASSESSMENT FILE FOR DETAILS BY INGREDIENT** Chilled product temperature on arrival < 5°C. Frozen product temperature on arrival <-18°c Check with calibrated probe. Correct Stock rotation Purchase from approved raw material & packaging suppliers Supplier Self Questionnaire & allergen cross contamination questionnaire completed and assessed for compliance Routine Supplier Audits Raw Material Specifications Certificate of Analysis per batch, if applicable All raw materials & packaging appropriately labelled with name, product, batch use by/BB & traceability. Visual inspection of delivery vehicle to ensure separation of product categories by space, if applicable, no evidence of foreign body contamination, strong odours, pest activity or chemical taints, damage to packaging/container. Check against agreed raw material and packaging specifications and certificate of analysis from supplier Process and policy for Goods In followed. Site Hygiene rules, policy and audits, Staff training, Hand swabs taken periodically, PPE, Correct stock rotation & site Traceability and labelling adhered to. Policy and Audits, Allergen Policy, Procedure, identification & segregation of materials. Staff Allergen training.	Y/N (assess microbial risk) Y Y

British Institute of Food Safety and Industrial Training, BIFSIT

HAZARD ANALYSIS

Step	Process Step	Hazard(s) Micro (including toxins), Chemical & Physical	Control Measures	Pre-requisite Y/N
3	Transfer Chilled to the Chiller area (Egg)	**Microbiological** (Spoilage; Yeast and Moulds /Pathogens: Salmonella spp., Listeria monocytogenes, Bacillus cereus, Enterobacteriaceae, Staphylococcus aureus, E.coli 1057, Clostridium perfingens, Coliforms, and their toxins) - **Presence & Growth** of spoilage and pathogens due to insufficient supplier & on site temperature controls during Chiller storage. - **Introduction by Contamination** of Staphylococcus from people - **Survival & growth** through insufficient area cleaning	Chiller store maintenance temperature of 0-5°c to maintain product temperature. Chilled <5°c. Temperature monitoring each batch using calibrated temperature probe, Site chiller temperature monitoring – continuous system and digital display readout. Planned maintenance on chiller. Allow for defrost air temperature to 12°c for no more than 30mins in a 4 - 6hr period. Chiller breakdown procedure Correct stock rotation, product use/by supplier and site traceability adhered to.	Y/N (assess microbial risk)
		Physical Contamination including foreign bodies from environmental debris: Glass & brittle materials Plastic String Metal Pests People Packaging Flaking Paint Metal Wood Egg Shell.	Cleaning schedules followed. Routine hand swabs and environmental & equipment swabbing Staff training, PPE Glass and brittle material policy and audits Metal policy and procedures PPM, Visual inspection Hygiene & housekeeping policy & audits Pest Control Wood and physical contamination policy and audits	Y
		Chemical Contamination **Cleaning chemical** taint residue from on site area cleaning **Deliberate Allergens :** Egg **Allergen risk of Cross contamination** from other products in the chiller	Food grade chemicals used and cleaning schedules followed, Staff training. No strong taints and odours. Allergen Policy, Procedure, identification & segregation of materials. Staff Allergen training FSA decision tree on risk of cross contamination at this step	Y/N (Allergens)

British Institute of Food Safety and Industrial Training, BIFSIT

HAZARD ANALYSIS

Step	Process Step	Hazard(s) Micro (Including toxins), Chemical & Physical	Control Measures	Pre-requisite Y/N
3a	Transfer Ambient Raw Materials & Packaging to Dry Stores area	**Microbiological** (Spoilage; Yeast and Moulds /Pathogens: Listeria monocytogenes, Bacillus cereus, Staphylococcus aureus, E.coli 1057, Coliforms, and their toxins) - **Presence of** Spoilage & Pathogens due to insufficient controls on site. - **Introduction by Contamination** of Staphylococcus from people during transfer (*CONSIDERED ONLY as these ingredients are considered Low Risk, Ambient, Low Aw & therefore the risk of sustaining any microbial growth is negligible*)	Correct stock rotation, product use/by supplier and site traceability adhered to. Hygiene & housekeeping Policy & procedures. Planned maintenance of area. Maintenance of dry Ambient Store <22°c Cleaning schedules followed. Routine hand swabs and environmental & equipment swabbing Staff training, PPE	Y
		Physical Contamination Including foreign bodies from Glass & brittle materials Plastic String Metal Pests including beetle/insects (SPI'S) People Packaging Flaking Paint Wood	Glass and brittle material policy and audits Metal policy and procedures PPM, Visual inspection Hygiene & housekeeping policy & audits Pest Control including Pheromone traps Wood and physical contamination policy and audits Food grade chemicals used and cleaning schedules followed, Staff training. No strong taints and odours.	Y
		Chemical Contamination **Cleaning chemical** taint residue from on site area cleaning **Deliberate Allergens** : Wheat Gluten, Nuts, Soy, Seeds, Peanuts **Rancidity** due to insufficient handling and stock rotation controls **Chemical Ink Solvents taints** from packaging	Allergen Policy, Procedure, identification & segregation of materials. Staff Allergen training Correct stock rotation, supplier products use by/BB & traceability adhered to Food grade packaging purchased from approved suppliers. Packaging specifications.	Y

British Institute of Food Safety and Industrial Training, BIFSIT

HAZARD ANALYSIS

Step	Process Step	Hazard(s) Micro (Including toxins), Chemical & Physical	Control Measures	Pre-requisite Y/N
3b	Transfer Frozen to the Freezer area (Puff Pastry, Danish Pastries, Tarts)	**Microbiological** (Spoilage; Yeast and Moulds /Pathogens: Salmonella spp, Listeria monocytogenes, Bacillus cereus, Enterobacteriaceae, Staphylococcus aureus, E.coli 1057, Clostridium perfingens, and their toxins) - **Presence & Growth** of spoilage and pathogens due to insufficient supplier & on site temperature controls during freezer storage. - **Introduction by Contamination** of Staphylococcus from people - **Survival & growth** through insufficient area cleaning **Physical Contamination** including foreign bodies from environmental debris: Glass & brittle materials Plastic String Metal Pests People Old Packaging Wood **Chemical Contamination** **Cleaning chemical** taint residue from freezer site area cleaning **Deliberate Allergens (Ingredients):** **Allergen risk of Cross contamination** from other products during on freezer storage	Freezer store maintenance temperature of -18°c - -23°c to maintain product temperature <-18°c Temperature monitoring once a day using calibrated temperature probe, Site freezer temperature monitoring – continuous system and digital display readout. Planned maintenance on freezer. Allow for defrost air temperature to -12°c for no more than 30mins in a 4 -6hr period. Freezer breakdown procedure Correct stock rotation, product use/by supplier and site traceability adhered to. Cleaning schedules followed. Routine hand swabs and environmental & equipment swabbing Staff training, PPE Glass and brittle material policy and audits Metal policy and procedures PPM, Visual inspection Hygiene & housekeeping policy & audits Pest Control Wood and physical contamination policy and audits Food grade chemicals used and cleaning schedules followed, Staff training. No strong taints and odours. Allergen Policy, Procedure, identification & segregation of materials. Staff Allergen training FSA decision tree on risk of cross contamination at this step	Y/N (assess microbial risk) Y Y/N (Allergens)

British Institute of Food Safety and Industrial Training, BIFSIT

HAZARD ANALYSIS

Step	Process Step	Hazard(s) Micro (including toxins), Chemical & Physical	Control Measures	Pre-requisite Y/N
4	De-box/Debag Ambient, Frozen, Chilled and Packaging	**Microbiological** (Spoilage; Yeast and Moulds /Pathogens: Salmonella spp., Listeria monocytogenes, Bacillus cereus, Enterobacteriaceae, Staphylococcus aureus, E.coli 1057, Clostridium perfingens, Coliforms, and their toxins) - **Presence & Growth** of spoilage and pathogens due to insufficient on site temperature and stock rotation controls during process - **Introduction by Contamination** of Staphylococcus from people	WIP out of chiller temperature <8°c for max 15 mins. Frozen if applicable kept >-15°c Check with calibrated probe. Line breakdown procedure adhered to. Correct stock rotation, product use/by supplier and site traceability adhered to. Planned maintenance of debagging/deboxing area.	Y
		Physical Contamination Including foreign bodies from Glass & brittle materials Plastic String Metal Pests including beetle/insects (SPI'S) People Packaging Flaking Paint Wood	Cleaning schedules followed. Routine hand swabs and environmental & equipment swabbing Staff training, PPE Glass and brittle material policy and audits Metal policy and procedures PPM, Visual inspection Hygiene & housekeeping policy & audits Pest Control including Pheromone traps Wood and physical contamination policy and audits	Y
		Chemical Contamination **Cleaning chemical** taint residue from on site area cleaning **Deliberate Allergens:** Wheat Gluten, Egg, Milk, Nuts, Soy, Seeds, Peanuts **Allergen risk of Cross contamination** from other products during debox/debagging **Rancidity** due to insufficient handling and stock rotation controls **Chemical Ink Solvents taints** from packaging	Food grade chemicals used and cleaning schedules followed, Staff training. No strong taints and odours. Allergen Policy, Procedure, identification & segregation of materials. Staff Allergen training Food grade packaging purchased from approved suppliers. Packaging specifications.	Y

British Institute of Food Safety and Industrial Training, BIFSIT

HAZARD ANALYSIS

Step	Process Step	Hazard(s) Micro (including toxins), Chemical & Physical	Control Measures	Pre-requisite Y/N
5	Transfer to Low Care Production Area	**Microbiological** (Spoilage; Yeast and Moulds /Pathogens: Salmonella spp., Listeria monocytogenes, Bacillus cereus, Enterobacteriaceae, Staphylococcus aureus, E.coli 1057, Clostridium perfingens, Coliforms, and their toxins) - **Presence & Growth** of spoilage and pathogens due to insufficient supplier & on site temperature and stock rotation controls during transfer - **Introduction by Contamination** of Staphylococcus from people	WIP out of chiller temperature <8°c & freezer <-15°c for max 15 mins. Check with calibrated probe. Line breakdown procedure adhered to. Correct stock rotation, product use/by supplier and site traceability adhered to. Cleaning schedules followed. Routine hand swabs and environmental & equipment swabbing Staff training, PPE	Y
		Physical Contamination Including foreign bodies from Glass & brittle materials Plastic String Metal Pests including beetle/insects (SPI'S) People Packaging Flaking Paint Wood	Glass and brittle material policy and audits Metal policy and procedures PPM, Visual inspection Hygiene & housekeeping policy & audits Pest Control including Pheromone traps Wood and physical contamination policy and audits	Y
		Chemical Contamination **Cleaning chemical** taint residue from on site area cleaning **Deliberate Allergens:** Wheat Gluten, Egg, Milk, Nuts, Soy, Seeds, Peanuts **Allergen risk of Cross contamination** from other products during transfer. **Rancidity** due to insufficient handling and stock rotation controls **Chemical Ink Solvents taints** from packaging	Food grade chemicals used and cleaning schedules followed, Staff training. No strong taints and odours. Allergen Policy, Procedure, identification & segregation of materials. Staff Allergen training Food grade packaging purchased from approved suppliers. Packaging specifications.	Y

British Institute of Food Safety and Industrial Training, BIFSIT

HAZARD ANALYSIS

Step	Process Step	Hazard(s) Micro (including toxins), Chemical & Physical	Control Measures	Pre-requisite Y/N
6	Transfer & Hold Frozen Material in CHILLER for Tempering/Defrosting (Puff pastry, semi-processed Danish, products.)	**Microbiological** (Spoilage; Yeast and Moulds /Pathogens: Salmonella spp, Listeria monocytogenes, Bacillus cereus, Enterobacteriaceae, Staphylococcus aureus, E.coli 1057, Clostridium perfingens, and their toxins) - **Presence & Growth** of spoilage and pathogens due to lack of control during tempering process within the chiller. - **Introduction by Contamination** of Staphylococcus from people - **Survival** through insufficient area cleaning **Physical Contamination** including foreign bodies from environmental debris: Glass & brittle materials Plastic String Metal Pests People Packaging Flaking Paint Wood **Chemical Contamination** **Cleaning chemical** taint residue from chiller site area cleaning **Deliberate Allergens (Ingredients):** Wheat Gluten, Egg, Milk **Allergen risk of Cross contamination** from other products during on tempering process in the chiller.	Chiller temperature of 0-5°c to control & maintain product core temperature during the tempering process. Product temp monitoring twice daily using calibrated temperature probe. Site chiller temperature monitoring – continuous system and digital display readout. Planned maintenance on chiller. Allow for defrost air temperature to 12°c for no more than 30mins in a 4 - 6hr period. Chiller breakdown procedure. In house Traceability & labelling policy and procedure Correct stock rotation, supplier products use by 0-3 days traceability adhered to Cleaning schedules followed. Routine hand swabs and environmental & equipment swabbing Staff training, PPE Glass and brittle material policy and audits Metal policy and procedures PPM, Visual inspection Hygiene & housekeeping policy & audits Pest Control Wood and physical contamination policy and audits Food grade chemicals used and cleaning schedules followed, Staff training. No strong taints and odours. Allergen Policy, Procedure, Identification & segregation of materials. Staff Allergen training FSA decision tree on risk of cross contamination at this step	Y/N (assess microbial risk) Y Y/N (Allergens)

British Institute of Food Safety and Industrial Training, BIFSIT

HAZARD ANALYSIS

Step	Process Step	Hazard(s) Micro (including toxins), Chemical & Physical	Control Measures	Pre-requisite Y/N
7	Batch Weigh ingredients	**Microbiological** (Spoilage; Yeast and Moulds /Pathogens: Salmonella spp., Listeria monocytogenes, Bacillus cereus, Enterobacteriaceae, Staphylococcus aureus, E.coli 1057, Clostridium perfingens, Coliforms, and their toxins) - **Presence & Growth** of spoilage and pathogens due to lack of time & temp control during weighing process. - **Introduction by Contamination** of Staphylococcus from people during the weighing and water	Process and recipe controls in place. Chilled WIP temperature <8°c for max 15 mins. Check with calibrated probe every batch Line breakdown procedure adhered to. Routine Water Point testing Correct stock rotation, supplier products use by/BB & traceability adhered to	Y
		Physical Contamination Including foreign bodies from Glass & brittle materials Plastic String Metal Pests including beetle/insects (SPI'S) People Packaging Flaking Paint Wood	Cleaning schedules followed. Routine hand swabs and environmental & equipment swabbing Staff training, PPE Glass and brittle material policy and audits Metal policy and procedures including knife control PPM, Visual inspection Hygiene & housekeeping policy & audits Pest Control including Pheromone traps Wood and physical contamination policy and audits	Y
		Chemical Contamination **Cleaning chemical** taint residue from on site area cleaning **Deliberate Allergens:** Wheat Gluten, Egg, Milk, Nuts, Soy, Seeds, Peanuts **Allergen risk of Cross contamination** from other products during the batch weighing and the equipment used previously **Rancidity** due to insufficient handling and stock rotation controls	Food grade chemicals used and cleaning schedules followed, Staff training. No strong taints and odours. Allergen Policy, Procedure, identification & segregation of materials. Staff Allergen training. FSA decision tree on risk of cross contamination at this step	Y/N (Allergens)

British Institute of Food Safety and Industrial Training, BIFSIT

HAZARD ANALYSIS

Step	Process Step	Hazard(s) Micro (including toxins), Chemical & Physical	Control Measures	Pre-requisite Y/N
8	Melting/Warming	**Microbiological** (Spoilage; Yeast and Moulds /Pathogens: Salmonella spp., Listeria monocytogenes, Bacillus cereus, Enterobacteriaceae, Staphylococcus aureus, E.coli 1057, Clostridium perfingens, Coliforms, and their toxins) - **Growth of** spoilage and pathogens due to incorrect recipe and on line process controls, in relation to time & temperatures. - **Introduction by Contamination** of Staphylococcus from people during the blending & mixing and rework - **Survival** through insufficient equipment cleaning **Physical Contamination** Including foreign bodies from Glass & brittle materials Plastic String Metal from equipment Pests including beetle/insects (SPI'S) People Packaging Flaking Paint Wood Dirt/Grit Product Lumps/crystallisation due to insufficient on site melting **Chemical Contamination** **Cleaning chemical** taint residue from on site area cleaning **Deliberate Allergens:** Wheat Gluten, Egg, Milk, Nuts, Soy, Seeds, Peanuts **Allergen risk of Cross contamination** from other products during the blending and the equipment used previously	Process controls in place refer to procedure Line breakdown procedure adhered to. Correct stock rotation, supplier & site products use by & traceability adhered to Cleaning schedules followed. Routine hand swabs and environmental & equipment swabbing Staff training, PPE Glass and brittle material policy and audits Metal policy and procedures including routine equipment and blade checks. PPM, Visual inspection Hygiene & housekeeping policy & audits Pest Control including Pheromone traps Wood and physical contamination policy and audits Food grade chemicals used and cleaning schedules followed, Staff training. No strong taints and odours. Allergen Policy, Procedure, identification & segregation of materials. Staff Allergen training FSA decision tree on risk of cross contamination at this step	Y/N (assess microbial risk) Y Y/N (Allergens)

British Institute of Food Safety and Industrial Training, BIFSIT

HAZARD ANALYSIS

Step	Process Step	Hazard(s) Micro (including toxins), Chemical & Physical	Control Measures	Pre-requisite Y/N
9	Blending & Mixing	**Microbiological** (Spoilage; Yeast and Moulds /Pathogens: Salmonella spp., Listeria monocytogenes, Bacillus cereus, Enterobacteriaceae, Staphylococcus aureus, E.coli 1057, Clostridium perfingens, Coliforms, and their toxins) - **Growth of** spoilage and pathogens due to incorrect recipe and on line process controls, in relation to time & temperatures. - **Introduction by Contamination** of Staphylococcus from people during the blending & mixing and rework - **Survival** through insufficient equipment cleaning **Physical Contamination** Including foreign bodies from Glass & brittle materials Plastic String Metal from equipment Pests including beetle/insects (SPI'S) People Packaging Flaking Paint Wood Dirt/Grit Product Lumps due to insufficient on site blending and mixing **Chemical Contamination** **Cleaning chemical** taint residue from on site area cleaning **Deliberate Allergens:** Wheat Gluten, Egg, Milk, Nuts, Soy, Seeds, Peanuts **Allergen risk of Cross contamination** from other products during the blending and the equipment used previously	Process controls in place. WIP temperature <8°c for max 15 mins. Check with calibrated probe every batch Line breakdown procedure adhered to. Correct stock rotation, supplier & site products use by & traceability adhered to Cleaning schedules followed. Routine hand swabs and environmental & equipment swabbing Staff training, PPE Glass and brittle material policy and audits Metal policy and procedures including routine equipment and blade checks. PPM, Visual inspection Hygiene & housekeeping policy & audits Pest Control including Pheromone traps Wood and physical contamination policy and audits Food grade chemicals used and cleaning schedules followed, Staff training. No strong taints and odours. Allergen Policy, Procedure, identification & segregation of materials. Staff Allergen training FSA decision tree on risk of cross contamination at this step	Y Y/N (assess metal risk) Y/N (Allergens)

British Institute of Food Safety and Industrial Training, BIFSIT

HAZARD ANALYSIS

Step	Process Step	Hazard(s) Micro (including toxins), Chemical & Physical	Control Measures	Pre-requisite Y/N
10	Cutting (if applicable – Danish, pastry))	**Microbiological** (Spoilage; Yeast and Moulds /Pathogens: Listeria monocytogenes, Salmonella spp., Bacillus cereus, Staphylococcus aureus, E.coli 1057, Coliforms, and their toxins) - **Growth of** spoilage and pathogens due to insufficient on line process controls, in relation to time & temperatures. - **Introduction by Contamination** of Staphylococcus from people during the cutting & forming - **Survival** through insufficient equipment cleaning	Process controls in place. WIP temperature <8°c for max 15 mins. Check with calibrated probe every batch Line breakdown procedure adhered to. Pastry rework policy and procedures Cleaning schedules followed. Routine hand swabs and weekly environmental & equipment swabbing Staff training, PPE	Y
		Physical Contamination Including foreign bodies from Glass & brittle materials Plastic Web fibres Metal from equipment Pests including beetle/insects (SPI'S) People Packaging Flaking Paint Wood	Glass and brittle material policy and audits Metal policy and procedures including routine equipment and blade checks. PPM, Visual inspection Hygiene & housekeeping policy & audits Pest Control including Pheromone trap audits Wood and physical contamination policy and audits	Y/N (assess metal risk)
		Chemical Contamination **Cleaning chemical** taint residue from on site area cleaning **Deliberate Allergens** : Wheat Gluten from Flour & Egg **Allergen risk of Cross contamination** from other products during the sheeting process	Food grade chemicals used and cleaning schedules followed, Staff training. No strong taints and odours. Allergen Policy, Procedure, identification & segregation of materials. Staff Allergen training	Y

British Institute of Food Safety and Industrial Training, BIFSIT

HAZARD ANALYSIS

Step	Process Step	Hazard(s) Micro (including toxins), Chemical & Physical	Control Measures	Pre-requisite Y/N
11	Deposit and/or Tray in readiness for oven baking	**Microbiological** Spoilage; Yeast and Moulds /Pathogens: Salmonella spp., Listeria monocytogenes, Bacillus cereus, Enterobacteriaceae, Staphylococcus aureus, E.coli 1057, Clostridium perfingens, Coliforms, and their toxins) - **Growth of** Spoilage & Pathogens due to incorrect on line process controls, in relation to time & temperatures. - **Introduction by Contamination** of Staphylococcus from people - **Survival and growth** through insufficient equipment cleaning **Physical Contamination** Including foreign bodies from Glass & brittle materials Plastic Web fibres Metal from tools and environment Pests including beetle/insects (SPI'S) People carbon Flaking Paint Wood **Chemical Contamination** **Cleaning chemical** taint residue from on site area cleaning **Deliberate Allergens:** Wheat Gluten, Egg, Milk, Nuts, Soy, Seeds, Peanuts **Allergen risk of Cross contamination** from other products during the process	WIP temperature <8°c max time 15mins Stock rotation & in house Traceability & labelling policy and procedure. Cleaning Schedules followed. Routine hand swabs and environmental & equipment swabbing Staff training, PPE Glass and brittle material policy and audits Metal policy and procedures including routine equipment and blade checks. PPM, Visual inspection Hygiene & housekeeping policy & audits Pest Control including Pheromone traps Wood and physical contamination policy and audits Food grade chemicals used and cleaning schedules followed, Staff training. No strong taints and odours. Allergen Policy, Procedure, identification & segregation of materials. Staff Allergen training	Y Y Y

British Institute of Food Safety and Industrial Training, BIFSIT

HAZARD ANALYSIS

Step	Process Step	Hazard(s) Micro (including toxins), Chemical & Physical	Control Measures	Pre-requisite Y/N
12	Proving (if applicable) (Danish's, Pastries)	**Microbiological** (Spoilage; Yeast and Moulds /Pathogens: Salmonella spp., Listeria monocytogenes, Bacillus cereus, Enterobacteriaceae, Staphylococcus aureus, E.coli 1057, Clostridium perfingens, Coliforms, and their toxins) - **Growth of** Spoilage & Pathogens due to incorrect proving, in relation to time & temperatures.	Process and recipe controls in place. Proving temperature of 30-35°c for 40mins approx OR variable time Temperature of each batch using a calibrated temperature probe. Line breakdown procedure adhered to.	Y/N (assess microbial risk)
		Physical Contamination including foreign bodies from environment and process of proving: Glass & brittle materials Old Product Metal from equipment & area Pests Plastic from utensils People Flaking Paint	Cleaning schedules followed. Routine hand swabs and weekly environmental & equipment swabbing Staff training, PPE Glass and brittle material policy and audits Metal policy and procedures and start-up checks PPM, Visual inspection Hygiene & housekeeping policy & audits Pest Control including Pheromone traps Wood and physical contamination policy and audits	Y
		Chemical Contamination **Cleaning chemical** taint residue from on site area cleaning **Deliberate Allergens:** Wheat Gluten, Egg, Milk, Nuts, Soy, Seeds, Peanuts **Allergen risk of Cross contamination** from other products during the proving process	Food grade chemicals used and cleaning schedules followed, Staff training. No strong taints and odours. Allergen Policy, Procedure, identification & segregation of materials. Staff Allergen training FSA decision tree on risk of cross contamination at this step	Y/N (Allergens)

British Institute of Food Safety and Industrial Training, BIFSIT

HAZARD ANALYSIS

Step	Process Step	Hazard(s) Micro (including toxins), Chemical & Physical	Control Measures	Pre-requisite Y/N
13	Oven Baking	**Microbiological** (Spoilage; Yeast and Moulds /Pathogens: Salmonella spp., Listeria monocytogenes, Bacillus cereus, Enterobacteriaceae, Staphylococcus aureus, E.coli 1057, Clostridium perfingens, Coliforms, and their toxins) - **Survival** of spollage and pathogens due to insufficient cooking temperature & time to achieve internal core temperature	Process and recipe controls in place. Variable baking temperatures (reference individual recipes) to achieve an internal core temperature >82°c for 30 secs. (>75°c for 2 mins cooking) Temperature of each batch using a calibrated temperature probe. Line breakdown procedure adhered to.	Y/N (assess microbial risk)
		Physical Contamination including foreign bodies from environment and process of cooking: Glass & brittle materials Old Product Metal from equipment & area Pests Plastic from utensils People Flaking Paint	Cleaning schedules followed. Routine hand swabs and environmental & equipment swabbing Staff training, PPE Glass and brittle material policy and audits Metal policy and procedures and start-up checks PPM, Visual Inspection Hygiene & housekeeping policy & audits Pest Control including Pheromone traps Wood and physical contamination policy and audits	Y
		Chemical Contamination **Cleaning chemical** taint residue from on site area cleaning **Deliberate Allergens:** Wheat Gluten, Egg, Milk, Nuts, Soy, Seeds, Peanuts **Allergen risk of Cross contamination** from other products during the baking and the oven used previously	Food grade chemicals used and cleaning schedules followed, Staff training. No strong taints and odours. Allergen Policy, Procedure, identification & segregation of materials. Staff Allergen training FSA decision tree on risk of cross contamination at this step	Y/N (Allergens)

British Institute of Food Safety and Industrial Training, BIFSIT

HAZARD ANALYSIS

Step	Process Step	Hazard(s) Micro (Including toxins), Chemical & Physical	Control Measures	Pre-requisite Y/N
14	Cooling and/or De-moulding (ambient environment)	**Microbiological** (Spoilage; Yeast and Moulds /Pathogens: Salmonella spp, Listeria monocytogenes, Bacillus cereus, Enterobacteriaceae, Staphylococcus aureus, E.coli 1057, Clostridium perfingens, and their toxins) - **Introduction by Contamination** of Staphylococcus from people - **Survival** through insufficient cleaning	Process and recipe controls in place Correct stock rotation and in house traceability labelling **Product, DOP + Use By 0-3 days & Internal traceability Code** until packed. **(Sponges Use By 1 day)** Planned Maintenance of chiller. Line breakdown procedure adhered to. Routine microbial indicator equipment swabbing & hand swabs Cleaning Schedules.	Y/N (assess microbial risk)
		Physical Contamination including foreign bodies from environmental debris: Glass & brittle materials Plastic String Metal Pests People Flaking Paint Wood	Staff training, PPE Glass and brittle material policy and audits Metal policy and procedures PPM, Visual inspection Hygiene & housekeeping policy & audits Pest Control Wood and physical contamination policy and audits Food grade chemicals used and cleaning schedules followed, Staff training. No strong taints and odours.	Y
		Chemical Contamination **Cleaning chemical** taint residue from chiller site area cleaning **Deliberate Allergens:** Wheat Gluten, Egg, Milk, Nuts, Soy, Seeds, Peanuts **Allergen risk of Cross contamination** from other products during the cooling process	Allergen Policy, Procedure, identification & segregation of materials. Staff Allergen training FSA decision tree on risk of cross contamination at this step	Y/N (Allergens)

British Institute of Food Safety and Industrial Training, BIFSIT

HAZARD ANALYSIS

Step	Process Step	Hazard(s) Micro (including toxins), Chemical & Physical	Control Measures	Pre-requisite Y/N
15	Tray, Stack & Label (if applicable)	**Microbiological** (Spoilage; Yeast and Moulds /Pathogens: Salmonella spp, Listeria monocytogenes, Bacillus cereus, Enterobacteriaceae, Staphylococcus aureus, E.coli 1057, Clostridium perfingens, and their toxins) - **Growth of** spoilage and pathogens due to insufficient on line process controls, in relation to times & temperatures. - **Introduction by Contamination** of Staphylococcus from people during the handling **Physical Contamination** Including foreign bodies from Glass & brittle materials Plastic Web Fibres Metal from area Pests including beetle/insects (SPI'S) People Packaging Flaking Paint Wood Old product **Chemical Contamination** **Cleaning chemical** taint residue from on site area and tray cleaning **Deliberate Allergens:** Wheat Gluten, Egg, Milk, Nuts, Soy, Seeds, Peanuts **Allergen risk of Cross contamination** from other products during the traying & boxing process **Chemical Ink Solvents taints** from packaging	Process controls in place. Temperature WIP temperature <8°c for max 15 mins. Check with calibrated probe every batch Internal Product Traceability & labelling policy and procedure: Line breakdown procedure adhered to. Cleaning schedules followed. Routine hand swabs and environmental & equipment swabbing Staff training, PPE Glass and brittle material policy and audits Metal policy and procedures. PPM, Visual inspection Hygiene & housekeeping policy & audits Pest Control including Pheromone trap audits Wood and physical contamination policy and audits Food grade chemicals used and cleaning schedules followed, Staff training. No strong taints and odours. Allergen Policy, Procedure, identification & segregation of materials. Staff Allergen training Food grade packaging purchased from approved suppliers. Packaging specifications.	Y Y Y

British Institute of Food Safety and Industrial Training, BIFSIT

HAZARD ANALYSIS

Step	Process Step	Hazard(s) Micro (including toxins), Chemical & Physical	Control Measures	Pre-requisite Y/N
16	Transfer to High Care Area	**Microbiological** Spoilage; Yeast and Moulds /Pathogens: Salmonella spp., Listeria monocytogenes, Bacillus cereus, Enterobacteriaceae, Staphylococcus aureus, E.coli 1057, Clostridium perfingens, Coliforms, and their toxins) - **Growth of** Spoilage & Pathogens due to incorrect on line process controls, in relation to time & temperatures. - **Introduction by Contamination** of Staphylococcus from people **Physical Contamination** Including foreign bodies from Glass & brittle materials Plastic Web fibres Metal from equipment Pests including beetle/insects (SPI'S) People Packaging Flaking Paint Wood **Chemical Contamination** **Cleaning chemical** taint residue from on site area cleaning **Deliberate Allergens:** Wheat Gluten, Egg, Milk, Nuts, Soy, Seeds, Peanuts **Allergen risk of Cross contamination** from other products during the transfer process	Environmental air conditioned Temperature in High Care <14°c Stock rotation & In house Traceability & labelling policy and procedure: Product, Traceability Coding Cleaning Schedules followed. Routine hand swabs and environmental & equipment swabbing Staff training, PPE Glass and brittle material policy and audits Metal policy and procedures including routine equipment and blade checks. PPM, Visual inspection Hygiene & housekeeping policy & audits Pest Control including Pheromone traps Wood and physical contamination policy and audits Food grade chemicals used and cleaning schedules followed, Staff training. No strong taints and odours. Allergen Policy, Procedure, identification & segregation of materials. Staff Allergen training	Y Y Y

British Institute of Food Safety and Industrial Training, BIFSIT

HAZARD ANALYSIS

Step	Process Step	Hazard(s) Micro (Including toxins), Chemical & Physical	Control Measures	Pre-requisite Y/N
17	Transfer & Hold in Chiller (if applicable) (Quality and/or Safety purposes)	**Microbiological** ((Spoilage; Yeast and Moulds /Pathogens: Salmonella spp, Listeria monocytogenes, Bacillus cereus, Enterobacteriaceae, Staphylococcus aureus, E.coli 1057, Clostridium perfingens, and their toxins) **Growth of** Spoilage & Pathogens due to incorrect temperature & time controls within the chiller - **Introduction by Contamination** of Staphylococcus from people	Product Temperature during chiller storage <5°C. Temperature monitoring once a day using calibrated temperature probe. Documented readings daily. Site chiller temperature 0-5°c monitoring – continuous system and digital display readout. Planned maintenance on chiller. Allow for defrost air temperature to 12°c for no more than 30mins in a 4hr period. Chiller breakdown procedure Product Traceability & labelling policy and procedure: Product, Traceability DOP+ Use By 3 - 17 days chilled/ambient	Y/N (assess microbial risk)
		Physical Contamination Including foreign bodies from Glass & brittle materials Plastic Metal from area Pests including beetle/insects (SPI'S) People Packaging Flaking Paint Wood	Cleaning schedules followed. Routine hand swabs and environmental & equipment swabbing Staff training, PPE Glass and brittle material policy and audits Metal policy and procedures. PPM, Visual inspection Hygiene & housekeeping policy & audits Pest Control Wood and physical contamination policy and audits	Y
		Chemical Contamination **Cleaning chemical** taint residue from on site area and tray cleaning **Deliberate Allergens:** Wheat Gluten, Egg, Milk, Nuts, Soy, Seeds, Peanuts **Allergen risk of Cross contamination** from other products during the storage in the chiller areas	Food grade chemicals used and cleaning schedules followed, Staff training. No strong taints and odours. Allergen Policy, Procedure, Identification & segregation of materials. Staff Allergen training FSA decision tree on risk of cross contamination at this step	Y/N (Allergens)

British Institute of Food Safety and Industrial Training, BIFSIT

HAZARD ANALYSIS

Step	Process Step	Hazard(s) Micro (Including toxins), Chemical & Physical	Control Measures	Pre-requisite Y/N
18	Cutting/Slicing (if applicable)	**Microbiological** (Spoilage; Yeast and Moulds /Pathogens: Salmonella spp., Listeria monocytogenes, Bacillus cereus, Enterobacteriaceae, Staphylococcus aureus, E.coli 1057, Clostridium perfingens, Coliforms, and their toxins) - **Presence & Growth** of spoilage and pathogens due to insufficient on site times & temperature, if applicable and stock rotation controls during transfer - **Introduction by Contamination** of Staphylococcus from people	Environmental air temperature <14°c. Stock rotation & in house Traceability & labelling policy and procedure: Product, Traceability Coding Cleaning schedules followed. Routine hand swabs and environmental & equipment swabbing Microbiological Air Plate testing	Y
		Physical Contamination Including foreign bodies from Glass & brittle materials Plastic String Metal Pests including beetle/insects (SPI'S) People Packaging Flaking Paint Wood	Staff training, PPE Glass and brittle material policy and audits Metal policy and procedures PPM, Visual inspection Hygiene & housekeeping policy & audits Pest Control including Pheromone traps Wood and physical contamination policy and audits Food grade chemicals used and cleaning schedules followed, Staff training. No strong taints and odours.	Y
		Chemical Contamination **Cleaning chemical** taint residue from on site area cleaning **Deliberate Allergens:** Wheat Gluten, Egg, Milk, Nuts, Soy, Seeds, Peanuts **Allergen risk of Cross contamination** from other products during transfer. **Chemical Ink Solvents taints** from packaging	Allergen Policy, Procedure, identification & segregation of materials. Staff Allergen training Food grade packaging purchased from approved suppliers. Packaging specifications.	Y

British Institute of Food Safety and Industrial Training, BIFSIT

HAZARD ANALYSIS

Step	Process Step	Hazard(s) Micro (including toxins), Chemical & Physical	Control Measures	Pre-requisite Y/N
19	Tray/box, Flow Wrap, Sleeve Packing, Stack & Label (if applicable)	**Microbiological** (Spoilage; Yeast and Moulds /Pathogens: Salmonella spp, Listeria monocytogenes, Bacillus cereus, Enterobacteriaceae, Staphylococcus aureus, E.coli 1057, Clostridium perfingens, and their toxins) - **Growth of** spoilage and pathogens due to insufficient on line process controls, in relation to times & temperatures. - **Introduction by Contamination** of Staphylococcus from people during the handling **Physical Contamination** Including foreign bodies from Glass & brittle materials Plastic Web Fibres Metal from area Pests including beetle/insects (SPI'S) People Packaging Flaking Paint Wood Old product **Chemical Contamination** **Cleaning chemical** taint residue from on site area and tray cleaning **Deliberate Allergens:** Wheat Gluten, Egg, Milk, Nuts, Soy, Seeds, Peanuts **Allergen risk of Cross contamination** from other products during the packing process **Chemical Ink Solvents taints** from packaging	Process controls in place. Temperature WIP chilled temperature <8°c for max 15 mins, if applicable. Check with calibrated probe every batch Product Traceability & labelling policy and procedure: Product, Traceability DOP+ Use By 3 – 17 days chilled or Ambient & BB 12 months frozen. Routine microbiological finished product testing and historical evidence of product safety. Line breakdown procedure adhered to. Cleaning schedules followed. Routine hand swabs and environmental & equipment swabbing Staff training, PPE Glass and brittle material policy and audits Metal policy and procedures. PPM, Visual Inspection Hygiene & housekeeping policy & audits Pest Control including Pheromone trap audits Wood and physical contamination policy and audits Food grade chemicals used and cleaning schedules followed, Staff training. No strong taints and odours. Allergen Policy, Procedure, identification & segregation of materials. Staff Allergen training Food grade packaging purchased from approved suppliers. Packaging specifications.	Y/N (assess microbial risk) Y Y

British Institute of Food Safety and Industrial Training, BIFSIT

HAZARD ANALYSIS

Step	Process Step	Hazard(s) Micro (Including toxins), Chemical & Physical	Control Measures	Pre-requisite Y/N
20	Transfer & Hold in Chiller Freezer OR Ambient	**Microbiological** ((Spoilage; Yeast and Moulds /Pathogens: Salmonella spp, Listeria monocytogenes, Bacillus cereus, Enterobacteriaceae, Staphylococcus aureus, E.coli 1057, Clostridium perfingens, and their toxins) **Growth of** Spoilage & Pathogens due to incorrect temperature & time controls within the chiller and freezer. - **Introduction by Contamination** of Staphylococcus from people **Physical Contamination** Including foreign bodies from Glass & brittle materials Plastic Metal from area Pests including beetle/insects (SPI'S) People Packaging Flaking Paint Wood **Chemical Contamination** **Cleaning chemical** taint residue from on site area and tray cleaning **Deliberate Allergens:** Wheat Gluten, Egg, Milk, Nuts, Soy, Seeds, Peanuts **Allergen risk of Cross contamination** from other products during the storage in the chiller/freezer/ambient areas	Product Temperature during chiller storage <5°C. Freezer store maintenance temperature of -18°c - -23°c to reduce temperature to <-12°c within 36hrs and thereafter maintain product temperature <-18°c Temperature monitoring once a day using calibrated temperature probe. Documented readings daily. Site chiller temperature 0-5°c monitoring – continuous system and digital display readout. Planned maintenance on chiller. Allow for defrost air temperature to 12°c for no more than 30mins in a 4-6hr period. Chiller breakdown procedure Planned maintenance on freezer. Allow for defrost air temperature to -12°c for no more than 30mins in a 4hr period. Freezer breakdown procedure Product Traceability & labelling policy and procedure: Product, Traceability DOP+ Use By 3 - 17 days chilled and ambient & BB 12 months frozen. Cleaning schedules followed. Routine hand swabs and environmental & equipment swabbing Staff training, PPE Glass and brittle material policy and audits Metal policy and procedures. PPM, Visual Inspection Hygiene & housekeeping policy & audits Pest Control Wood and physical contamination policy and audits Food grade chemicals used and cleaning schedules followed, Staff training. No strong taints and odours. Allergen Policy, Procedure, identification & segregation of materials. Staff Allergen training FSA decision tree on risk of cross contamination at this step	Y/N (assess microbial risk) Y Y/N (Allergens)

British Institute of Food Safety and Industrial Training, BIFSIT

HAZARD ANALYSIS

Step	Process Step	Hazard(s) Micro (including toxins), Chemical & Physical	Control Measures	Pre-requisite Y/N
21	Despatch OR Customer Collection (*Any hazard occurring after pick up are not the responsibility of*)	**Microbiological** (Spoilage; Yeast and Moulds /Pathogens: Salmonella spp, Listeria monocytogenes, Bacillus cereus, Enterobacteriaceae, Staphylococcus aureus, E.coli 1057, Clostridium perfingens, and their toxins) - **Growth of** Spoilage & Pathogens due to loss of temperature controls during despatch & transfer **Physical Contamination** including foreign bodies from environmental debris: Glass & brittle materials Metal Pests Wood People **Chemical Contamination** **Cleaning chemical** taint residue from vehicle cleaning **Deliberate Allergens:** Wheat Gluten, Egg, Milk, Nuts, Soy, Seeds, Peanuts **Allergen risk of Cross contamination** from other products during the despatch	Product packs to be frozen prior to despatch. <-18°c Frozen temperature of despatch vehicle. <-18°C Chilled packs to be <5°c and vehicle <5°c - Routine maintenance of company despatch vehicle. Cleaning Schedules followed. Adequate space separation or total despatch isolation between different food categories and raw and cooked products In house Traceability & labelling policy and procedure: Product, Traceability Code, Use by 3 – 14 days chilled and ambient and BB + 12 months Frozen Vehicle breakdown procedure. Despatch policy and procedures Hygiene Audits Cleaning schedules, Training, visual inspection. Glass and brittle material policy and audits Metal detection Policy & Procedure. Pest Control. PPE, Staff Training Food grade chemicals used and cleaning schedules followed, Staff training. Allergen Policy, Procedure, identification & segregation of materials. Staff Allergen training.	Y/N (assess microbial risk) Y Y

British Institute of Food Safety and Industrial Training, BIFSIT

HAZARD ANALYSIS

Step	Process Step	Hazard(s) Micro (including toxins), Chemical & Physical	Control Measures	Pre-requisite Y/N
22	Customer Returns	**Microbiological** (Spoilage; Yeast and Moulds /Pathogens: Salmonella spp, Listeria monocytogenes, Bacillus cereus, Enterobacteriaceae, Staphylococcus aureus, E.coli 1057, Clostridium perfingens, and their toxins) - **Growth & contamination** of spoilage and pathogens due to insufficient on site customer controls during handling/storage & Returns.	Return vehicle conditions <-18°c to maintain product core temperature <-18°c or <8°c to maintain product core at <5°c Isolation and identification during customer storage and during return transportation to ensure no risk of cross contamination. Ambient products N/A	N (Customer policy and pre-requisites unknown for returns)
		- **Physical Contamination** including foreign bodies from transportation, environmental & pallets debris: Wood Glass & Brittle Materials Pests String Packaging People **Visual spoilage** due to excessive temperatures and humidity during customer storage and return vehicle	Wood and physical contamination policy and audits Routine maintenance & hygiene Audits of vehicle, Staff Training , , Hygiene policy Pest Control & routine audits Vehicle breakdown procedure. Despatch policy and procedures Visual inspection of vehicle on arrival	N
		Chemical Contamination Cleaning Chemical taints & residue in vehicle and at customer storage site Deliberate Allergen on Finished Products and risks of cross contamination from other products and customers.	Food grade chemicals used and cleaning schedules followed, Staff training. Allergen Policy, packaging & labelling identification and segregation. Staff Allergen training.	N

British Institute of Food Safety and Industrial Training, BIFSIT

The 'Likelihood' and 'Severity' of hazards, other than those covered by the Pre-requisite programme, needs to be assessed to determine, if, after using the decision tree process the Hazards are true Critical Control Points or lesser Control Points.
Most risk analysis systems measure 2 aspects of the hazard:
Likelihood – how likely the hazard is going to cause harm or injury.
Severity – how severe are the consequences of the hazard, if it occurred.

The risk is determined by giving a score to each of these aspects and reading the scores against a matrix.

Dealing with food safety, the scores are as follows:

Likelihood of Hazard	Score
Common occurrence	1
Known to occur *(e.g. has happened at our premises before)*	2
Could occur *(e.g. we have heard about it happening elsewhere)*	3
Not likely to occur	4
Practically impossible	5

Severity of Hazard & Vulnerability of those exposed	Score
Can cause fatality	1
Can lead to serious illness / harm	2
Can cause a product recall	3
Can generate a customer complaint	4
Not of significance	5

Having obtained the 2 scores, they should then be read against the matrix below:

Severity → / Likelihood ↓	1	2	3	4	5
1	1	3	6	10	15

2	2	5	9	14	19
3	4	8	13	18	22
4	7	12	17	21	24
5	11	16	20	23	25

Matrix readings in RED area are significant hazards and will be a CCP if defined by the Decision Tree.

Matrix readings in GREEN area are deemed less significant. If the Decision Tree Process identifies the hazard at the process step as a CCP, the HACCP team can change output from a CCP to a Control Point as the hazard has been shown to be of lesser significance.

Findings are recorded on the Decision Tree Matrix.

CODEX ALIMENTARIUS STEP 7 Principle 2 Decision Tree

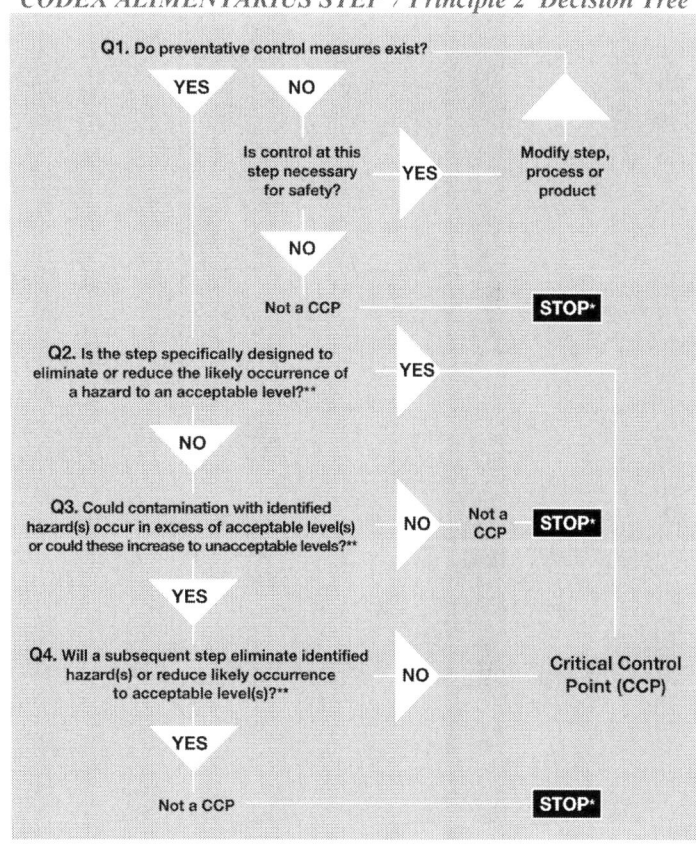

Q1. Do preventative control measures exist?

- YES
- NO → Is control at this step necessary for safety?
  - YES → Modify step, process or product
  - NO → Not a CCP — **STOP***

Q2. Is the step specifically designed to eliminate or reduce the likely occurrence of a hazard to an acceptable level?**
- YES → **STOP***
- NO ↓

Q3. Could contamination with identified hazard(s) occur in excess of acceptable level(s) or could these increase to unacceptable levels?**
- NO → Not a CCP — **STOP***
- YES ↓

Q4. Will a subsequent step eliminate identified hazard(s) or reduce likely occurrence to acceptable level(s)?**
- NO → Critical Control Point (CCP)
- YES → Not a CCP — **STOP***

© British Institute of Food Safety & Industrial Training 2017

PROCESS STEP & HAZARD	Q2. If Yes this Step is a CCP If No move to Q3.	JUSTIFICATION FOR DECISION	Q3. If No this Step is not a CCP If yes move on to Q4	JUSTIFICATION FOR DECISION	Q4. If Yes this step is not a CCP If No- this Step is a CCP	JUSTIFICATION FOR DECISION	Likelihood	Severity	Rating	CCP No
2. Goods In Inspection - Microbial Growth	Yes	This step is specific to a temperature check which will accept or reject a batch of delivered chilled or frozen					3	4	18 (Due to cooking/ baking step)	Down Grade to CP
3 Transfer and Hold in Chiller - Microbial Growth	No	Temperature in the fridge will not reduce or eliminate microbial growth within the egg, just slow down the process of growth for a period of time.	Yes/No	There is slight risk of microbial growth on the chilled material due to the uncooked nature of the product	Yes	The subsequent baking processes will reduce or eliminate the hazard if present	3	4	18	N/A
3b Transfer & Hold in FREEZER Microbial growth	No	Freezing temperatures will not reduce or eliminate the hazard, it will only suspend any microbial growth if present	No	Microbial growth cannot occur during freezing, unless >-12°c			5	4	23	N/A
6 Transfer & Hold in CHILLER for Tempering Microbial growth	No	Tempering in the chiller is designed to control the risk of microbial growth not reduce or eliminate it.	Yes	There is a slight risk of microbial growth on the materials when tempering in the chiller.	Yes/No	There is a baking step for most materials however some materials have no subsequent step that will reduce or eliminate the	4	4	21	CP

| | | | | | microbial hazard. | | | | |

PROCESS STEP & HAZARD	Q2. If Yes this Step is a CCP If No move to Q3.	JUSTIFICATION FOR DECISION	Q3. If No this Step is not a CCP If yes move on to Q4	JUSTIFICATION FOR DECISION	Q4. If Yes this step is not a CCP If No- this Step is a CCP	JUSTIFICATION FOR DECISION	Likelihood	Severity	Rating	CCP No
8. Melting/Warming	No	This is to change the format of the product for quality reasons only ie; melting chocolate to assist blending together.	No	The melting has a limited shelf life for quality reasons and therefore the risk of any microbial growth is negligible			4	4	21	N/A
9. Blending & Mixing Metal	No	This is the blending and mixing using metal blades	No	There are start up/end checks on line/machines & equipment. Metal risk assessments determining further controls necessary			4	3	17	CP
10. Cutting Metal	No	This is the dough sheeting and cutting of which there is a risk of metal contamination from the blades for cutting	No	There are start up/end checks on line/machines & equipment. Metal risk assessments determining further controls necessary			4	3	17	CP
12. Proving - Microbial growth	No	This step is to allow the material to rise in shape prior to baking	Yes	There is a risk of microbial growth if the time and temperatures are not adhered to correctly	Yes	A subsequent Baking step will reduce or eliminate the hazard if applicable	3	4	18	N/A

| PROCESS STEP & | Q2. If Yes this | | Q3. If No this | | Q4. If Yes | | Likelihood | Severity | Rating | |

HAZARD	Step is a CCP If No move to Q3.	JUSTIFICATION FOR DECISION	Step is not a CCP If yes move on to Q4	JUSTIFICATION FOR DECISION	this step is not a CCP If No- this Step is a CCP	JUSTIFICATION FOR DECISION				CCP No
13 Oven Baking - Microbial survival	Yes	Cooking will reduce or eliminate any micro-organisms present					2	2	5	CCP
14 Cooling - Microbial Survival	No	This step is to cool the sponges, pastries etc which is carried out in an ambient environment	No	The nature of the material at this step is presently not classed as High risk Perishable therefore with minimal risk of any microbial growth			4	4	21	N/A
17 & 20 Store in Product Chiller (Part Processed & Finished product) - Microbial growth	No	Temperature in the fridge will not reduce or eliminate microbial growth on the finished packed products, just slow down the process of growth for a period of time.	Yes	There is a slight risk that any micro-organisms remaining could grow to unacceptable levels (although products are not considered high risk perishable and some are chilled for quality reasons)	No	There is no subsequent process step that will prevent the growth of bacteria. This step is a CCP.	3	3	13	Team would like to keep this a CCP
19 Finished Product Labelling - Microbial growth	No	Labelling will inform the consumer of the safe use by date prior to the possibility of any microbial growth if applicable	No	Contamination risks are low due to the onsite pre-requisites to ensure compliance. The nature of the products is not considered high risk perishable due to the low Aw		It is the responsibility of the consumer to adhere to the safety details on purchase	4	4	21	N/A

| PROCESS | Q2. | Q3. | Q4. | Likelihood | Severity | Rating | |

STEP & HAZARD	If Yes this Step is a CCP If No move to Q3.	JUSTIFICATION FOR DECISION	If No this Step is not a CCP If yes move on to Q4	JUSTIFICATION FOR DECISION	If Yes this step is not a CCP If No- this Step is a CCP	JUSTIFICATION FOR DECISION				CCP No
20 Transfer & Hold in FREEZER - Microbial growth	No	Freezing temperatures will not reduce or eliminate the hazard, it will only suspend any microbial growth if present	No	Microbial growth cannot occur during freezing, unless >-12°c			5	4	23	N/A
21 Despatch (own vehicle & delivery & Chilled only) - Microbial Growth	No	The process of despatch will not reduce or eliminate the amount of Bacteria present on the product.	Yes	During despatch there is a slight risk of the microbial growth on the product if stored as chilled, due to loss of temp control & risk of cross contamination (although products are not considered high risk perishable due to Aw)	No	There is no subsequent process step that is under the control of Barons that will prevent the growth of bacteria. This step is a CCP.	3	3	13	Team would like to keep this as a CCP
20. Customer Return on Rejection Microbiological/ Physical/Chemical	No	The process of product return will not reduce or eliminate the hazards present.	Yes	Unknown controls during transport and return to the factory.	Yes	Reject / Destroy products on their return.	5	5	25	N/A

CODEX ALIMENTARIUS STEP 8/9/10 Principle 3/4/5

SUMMARY of CCP's: HACCP PLAN FOR: THE MANUFACTURE & PACKING OF SPONGE BASES, DANISH, MUFFINS, BISCUITS & PUDDINGS

Process Step & Hazard	CCP No.	Control Measures Standards and Tolerances	Monitoring				Corrective Actions		
			Procedure	Frequency	Responsibility	Records	Procedure	Responsibility	Records
13 Baking - Microbiological	3	Cooking temperature Variable (Ref to recipes) to achieve an internal core temperature for baking >82°c for 30 secs. (>75°c for 2 mins cooking)	Product temperature taken with a disinfected calibrated temperature probe on removing from the oven. Oven display time & temperatures recorded	Each Batch cooked	Operator	PCS 0003 PCS 0004 SOP 0003	Inform Manager/ Return to max cooking temperature/Reject batch	Operator	PCS 0003 PCS 0004 SOP 0003 Incident Report PCS 0008 SOP 0008

SUMMARY of CCP's: HACCP PLAN FOR: THE MANUFACTURE & PACKING OF SPONGE BASES, DANISH, MUFFINS, BISCUITS & PUDDINGS

Process Step & Hazard	CCP No.	Control Measures Standards and Tolerances	Monitoring Procedure	Monitoring Frequency	Monitoring Responsibility	Monitoring Records	Corrective Actions Procedure	Corrective Actions Responsibility	Corrective Actions Records
17 & 20 Transfer & hold in Chiller (Part-Processed & Finished Products) - Microbiological	2	Chilled storage temperatures. 0-5°C. Finished Product temp Monitoring to be <5°c taken using a disinfected calibrated temperature probe. Correct stock rotation and in house traceability labelling. Planned Maintenance of chiller. Allow for defrost chill storage air temp of up to 12°C for no more than 30 minutes in a 4 hour period. Routine micro swabbing.	Manual check of product temp using a calibrated disinfected probe. Physical check against digital	Min 2 x Products & 1 x Air Temp Daily Daily	Operator	PCS 0002 SOP 0002	Reduce chill room temperature. Move product to another chill store. Inform Manager, Review cause of the problem. Retrain Operators Destroy suspect product.	Operator	PCS 0002 SOP 0002 Incident Report PCS 0008 SOP 0008
20 Despatch (Own vehicle, **Chilled only**) - Microbiological	5	Chilled delivery vehicle temperatures. <5°C. Finished Product packs temperature monitoring at loading to be <5°c Routine hygiene and housekeeping checks of despatch vehicle.	Manual check of product temp using a calibrated disinfected probe Empty vehicle temp recorded. Product temp recorded at delivery.	Sample from each load. prior to loading Each delivery	Operator Manager & Driver	PCS 0006 SOP 0006	Withhold despatch until product reaches required temp. Review cause of the problem. Abort loading until vehicle reaches required temp. Return product, Isolate and place on hold in chiller to assess situation. Reject or Release.	Operator, Manager & Driver	PCS 0006 SOP 0006 Incident Report PCS 0008 SOP 0008

© British Institute of Food Safety & Industrial Training 2017

Printed in Great Britain
by Amazon